Top Marketing Tactics That Boost Sales

Customers Don't Just Pour in Online, They Abound Offline Too!

By: Jeff Collins

9781635019889

I0500322

PUBLISHERS NOTES

Disclaimer – Speedy Publishing LLC

This publication is intended to provide helpful and informative material. It is not intended to diagnose, treat, cure, or prevent any health problem or condition, nor is intended to replace the advice of a physician. No action should be taken solely on the contents of this book. Always consult your physician or qualified health-care professional on any matters regarding your health and before adopting any suggestions in this book or drawing inferences from it.

The author and publisher specifically disclaim all responsibility for any liability, loss or risk, personal or otherwise, which is incurred as a consequence, directly or indirectly, from the use or application of any contents of this book.

Any and all product names referenced within this book are the trademarks of their respective owners. None of these owners have sponsored, authorized, endorsed, or approved this book.

Always read all information provided by the manufacturers' product labels before using their products. The author and publisher are not responsible for claims made by manufacturers.

This book was originally printed before 2014. This is an adapted reprint by Speedy Publishing LLC with newly updated content designed to help readers with much more accurate and timely information and data.

Speedy Publishing LLC

40 E Main Street, Newark, Delaware, 19711

Contact Us: 1-888-248-4521

Website: http://www.speedypublishing.co

REPRINTED Paperback Edition: 9781635019889:

Manufactured in the United States of America

DEDICATION

I wrote this book in loving memory of my aunt, Mary. You have been my mother and my best friend. Your memory will live forever.

TABLE OF CONTENTS

Chapter 1- Back to Basics: Traditional Offline Marketing That Work Wonders

Don't think of these methods as too simple or mundane. They are very effective when done right and combined with other techniques in this report.

1)   Classified Ads

This is something everyone should be testing in some form or another. It's great for lead generations. You should still have a strong benefit-driven headline and a clear call to action. Free reports work very well with classifieds. My local paper, the Hartford Courant even has an ongoing deal of 3 lines for 3 days – for free! Even adding more lines only ends up costing a few bucks.

With a price like that, there's no reason anyone with a website should not be testing ways to draw traffic to the site with classifieds.

2)   Direct Mail

Nothing beats direct response when it comes to results-driven proven advertising. And messages sent directly to your highly targeted market via direct mail can deliver a terrific return on investment (ROI) when tested properly. There's a wealth of information on direct marketing by Michel Fortin, David Garfinkel, Gary Halbert, Dan Kennedy, and many more experts.

3)   Postcards

Yes, postcards are a form of direct mail, but it warrants its own category. Postcards are cheaper to produce and mail than full-blown direct mail packages or sales letters, and they are great for generating leads. Like classified ads, a free report or free gift often works well here. Postcards are also a great way to stay in touch with your customers and prospects, and they also work well as part of a sequence of mailings. A good place to go for customized postcards is http://www.usps.com (the US Postal Service website), because the USPS has partnered with a company that will print and mail your postcards for you! Best of all, you only pay for the postage fees (i.e. FREE printing costs). Hint: be sure to include yourself on the mailing list so you can get your own mailing as well.

4)   Yellow Pages

Another great resource that is often underutilized or used ineffectively. Yellow page ads are great because when someone sees your ad, they are already in the market for your product or service. Yellow page ads need to be benefits-driven, with your

Unique Selling Proposition (USP) stated clearly and boldly (remember, this is the one place where your prospects will see your ad alongside all of your competitors). You want your ad to stand out from the clutter. Use a direct response type of ad, and again, free gifts or premiums work well here.

Gary Halbert has written about yellow pages several times in his newsletter. To find them easily, just enter the following search at Google: site:thegaryhalbertletter.com +"yellow page"

5)   Space Ads

If you're going to do a space ad, it will generally get better results if you use the same layout as the editorials. Use the same font styles and sizes for the headline, body, etc. If the newspaper uses 2 columns per article on the page your ad will appear, use 2 columns in your ad. If they use 3 columns, you use 3. The "advertorial" approach almost always does better than traditional space ads that scream "ad."

A great way to get very low costs space ads is to use what's known as remnant, or standby advertising. Enter the following search in Google to see what I mean and to learn more:

site:thegaryhalbertletter.com +"Nancy Jones"

And you'll learn to experiment in many creative ways to find out what works for you. A local advertising paper, the Rare Reminder here in the Hartford area, has classified ads and space ads. But I noticed that one "stone and mulch" company has their space ad featured upside-down in every weekly issue. At first I thought it was a mistake. But after seeing it upside-down week after week, I suspected they found that their upside-down ad stands out from the clutter. People think it's a mistake and read it. Yes, it's a gimmick. Would I do it? Only if it tested positively and maybe it has for these folks. Food for thought.

6)   Radio/TV/Infomercials

You might be surprised how inexpensive you can get these types of slots, especially if you use remnant advertising. Study the best infomercials, for example (the ones you see over and over again...they must be working or they wouldn't keep airing them), to get some ideas on how they are constructed.

7)   Flyers

Who says you can't hire a high school student to stuff mailboxes or stick 'em under windshields? Obviously if you are selling a high-priced financial course, it would be better to target the windshields of a fancy hotel than your local Wal-Mart. And I believe the US Postal Service also prints them for you like they do postcards if you want to mail them. Check out http://www.usps.com

8)   Networking

Your local Chamber of Commerce, trade shows, seminars, and anywhere your prospects hang out are all good opportunities for networking. In many cases, the hotel bar the night before the seminar is the best opportunity for making contacts. It's usually more effective to try to capture contacts and leads than to try to close a sale on the spot, so get your elevator speech ready and have plenty of business cards on hand.

9)   Telemarketing

Remember the "Do Not Call" list only applies to consumers, so if you do any kind of business to business selling, telemarketing is a viable marketing method you can use effectively. Also, the "Do Not Call" list may not apply to you with your customers or if you already have a relationship with your prospects.

10)   A Trade Show Booth

A great place to capture leads. Again, a free report or gift does wonders. When you get a long line waiting at your booth, many people will stop by just to see what the fuss is about. Make your sales materials and sales people benefit-driven. Remember what your prospects are thinking: "What's in it for me?"

11)   Blimps, Banners, and Billboards

If it's zoned for advertising and it's blank, you have an opportunity.

12)   Door Hangers

Those same high school students can help you with door hangers as well.

13)   Circulars

Again, high school students can also help you hand out circulars, post them on community bulletin boards, on telephone poles, wherever. You can make a donation to your local church and ask them if you can leave a stack at their next bake sale or bingo event. And certainly you can arrange to have your circular included in your local newspaper or community paper. For your money, circulars are very inexpensive to print and distribute.

14)   Card Decks

These stacks of index cards are mailed to targeted audiences. Each deck can contain anywhere from 50 to 200 cards or so, each with an advertisement or coupon. They may also double as a business reply card on back. Since your ad is mixed in with tons of others, it's especially important to have a great headline and layout that will stand out from the clutter.

Card decks are inexpensive because all of the advertisers are sharing the cost of the mailing. They can cost as little as three cents a prospect for large mailings. Even for smaller mailings, they are generally cheap, which is good for testing.

Make sure you choose your audience wisely. Card decks are great for targeting a niche. Free reports or books work especially well here, because the person flipping through the cards will be attracted to the word "FREE." As always, make sure there is a clear call to action. Multiple methods of response usually work better than a single method. For example, they can drop the card in the mail, call a free recorded message, go to your website, etc. And you may have some options with remnant space, so always try to negotiate a lower price (how hard is it for them to stick another card in their mailing...their costs are incremental and their profit is high even on remnant rates).

A couple other tips: When you see repeat advertisers in a deck, you have a pretty good idea that the deck is working for that ad. If that ad also targets your niche market, it may be a good one to test in. Also, test with copy that you already know works.

15)   Value-Packs

Similar to card decks, "value-packs" are little booklets with multiple ads. They are mostly used with coupons, rather than business reply cards.

16)   Ad Magazines

You've seen them - magazines that are little more than a collection of space ads. They are usually local, and the ads in them usually aren't direct response. By putting your direct response ad there, you stand out over all the other ads. But the downside is that these magazines tend to be less niche-focused (although there are certainly exceptions, with the real estate and automobile-themed magazines and newspapers).

17)   Catalogues

Your catalog doesn't have to look like L.L. Bean or the like to be effective. A good one to study with respect to the ads themselves is the J. Peterman catalogue.

Here's a good way to start small and work up from there in developing a good catalogue:

a) Try a simple double-sided flyer first and test response.

b) Make sure you locate highly targeted lists, as the wasted cost of mailings is going to be your biggest expense.

c) Continue to expand, test, and tweak. Test everything—your layout, your copy, your prices—until you find the best combination.

CHAPTER 2- CREATIVITY MATTERS IN OFFLINE MARKETING

18)   Package Inserts

If you're going to mail out a product or package to a customer anyway, always tuck a sales letter for another product in the package. It won't cost you anymore, and when your customer receives that package, he or she will be pleased with the product (assuming your product isn't junk) and be more favorable towards another purchase from you. You can also joint venture with other companies that target your niche market and get them to include your insert when shipping their product.

19)   Mini-seminars

These are excellent means of bundling up all your products and services then selling them from the platform. It's very inexpensive to rent a hall and put on a 2 hour presentation for your target market on something that interests them. You position yourself as the expert, and you get to pitch your products and services. Be sure to record the event and offer it to other prospects that may not be able to attend the presentation in person.

Speakers don't get paid, but still make money by pitching their products. It works, and anyone who doesn't have one or more of these planned is missing out of a lot of extra potential income.

20)   Teleseminars

Basically a conference call, we've all probably been on many of them. Some have organized them and have been speakers. They can be pure content (i.e. no obvious pitches) for strengthening social proof and building up anticipation for a new product to be released in the future. They can be a mixture of content and pitch. You can even arrange a series of them as a tele-course and charge big money to attend (Marc Goldman and Jay Abraham did this with a six-month long series, one per month, on joint ventures and deal making).

21)   Voice Broadcasts

A very under-utilized technique. If you have an existing relationship with your customers or prospects, the Do Not Call list does not apply. That sets the stage for a great way to call thousands of your customers simultaneously when they are most likely to be away from home. You simply upload your customer's phone numbers, record the message you want to leave, and the technology does the rest.

Example: "Hi, this is John Smith. Sorry I missed you, but I wanted to let you know that our firesale is ending tomorrow..."

Voice broadcasts work best when they are part of a sequence.

Example: "Hi, this is John Smith calling, from Smith Publishing. I'm sorry that I missed you, but I wanted to let you know about a valuable letter and free gift we're sending to your home. You should be getting it in the next day or two. Just look for the bright blue envelope..."

22)   Gift Certificates

It's generally known that people will usually spend more than the gift certificate amount. So if you operate a jewelry store, and you mail your customers a free no-obligation $25 gift certificate, it's usually a very sound investment. Most restaurant owners already know that people generally don't dine alone, so by giving your customers a free gift certificate; they're bound to bring in others who will spend more money on food and drinks. A good variation on this formula is the free birthday dinner. Generally, nobody is going to come in on their birthday and eat their free dinner by themselves. They're going to bring friends, relatives, you get the idea.

Here's a great way to use gift certificates to get referrals: Send a letter to your customers with three gift certificates. One they can use for themselves and the other two they can give away to friends or relatives. They keep your customers happy (and happy customers are more likely to speak highly of you to others) and they compound that fact by letting your customers give the certificates to others, to whom they will sing your praises. It's like a tell-a-friend script on steroids!

23)   Coupons

Like gift certificates, coupons are also a great way to "touch" your customers and bring them back into your store (or website or whatever).

24)   Contests

The sandwich chain Subway recently had a scratch-off contest, but you had to go online to see if you were a winner. Contests are a great way to get leads and generate sales. Here's a tip: always include an unadvertised "second place" that everyone who didn't win will get. Joe Vitale did that last year, and used an email and voice broadcast to announce your "second place" prize. I would have included a sequence of direct mail as well, but the premise is the same.

Also, the Nathan's hot dog eating contest is a great example of using their product in the contest itself. If your product or service lends itself well to this approach, consider testing it.

25)   Celebrity Endorsements

They aren't as expensive as you might think (unless you try to get Sean Connery or Tom Cruise). The key is that you need to use celebrities that your target market recognizes as such. So Tony Rice would make a great celebrity for bluegrass and acoustic guitar enthusiasts. Not so much for gardening fans.

26) CD Sales letter

People generally won't read 90 minutes worth of copy, but they will listen to it. The perceived value is much higher than a traditional sales letter as well. They can listen to it in their cars; on their Walkman (although today everyone has an iPod...why not use a podcast instead?). The point is that you can cram in a lot more information. You can do testimonials in their own voices, have sound effects or music. Anything to help advance the sale.

27) Thank You Letters

Whether you send gift certificates, coupons, a 2 for 1 special, a free gift, or just a friendly thank you letter to stay on your customer's radar screen, these types of letters are memorable and encourage your customers to send you referrals. As always, these types of letters should be personalized, and never use a mailing address letter on the envelope.

Example:

Dear Mr. Smith,

I hope you are very pleased with your recent purchase of my quality artwork. May it bring much viewing pleasure for you and your family for years to come.

Being an independent artist, I truly appreciate your business! I really want to personally thank you!

You should know that a recent painting I did was auctioned locally for more than $10,000.00! My work is featured at local art shows, and my original Silent Tempest painting has been on display in the Wadsworth Atheneum in Hartford since 1998. That means if you hold onto your painting, you'll likely see its value increase considerably.

As you may know, I also paint custom portraits, landscapes, abstract art, and theme-based artwork from your choice of subjects.

What does that mean for you?

Good question. I just moved into a new, more spacious studio, and I'm having a special sale just for my best customers. Here's what I want you to do (you'll love this): call me right away for a absolutely FREE, no obligation quote on any custom painting you'd like me to do for you. But...

Don't tell me you have this letter until after I give you my free no-hassle quote. Only then tell me that you have this letter, and I'll knock off an additional 21% off of my already ridiculously low price.

That way you'll know for sure I haven't "padded" my price just to give the appearance of a sale. I'm going to let you trick me!

Why would I do this? Simple. I want you as a customer for life. Most of my customers come back again and again, because they love my inspiration and extraordinary use of colors. And they appreciate the fact that no other local artist enjoys an appreciation on the value of their paintings as I do.

So call me today at (555) 555-5555 for your FREE quote.

Very Truly Yours,

John Artist

P.S. Remember, call me right away to take advantage of this most exclusive offer for my best customers only.

P.P.S. Also, don't tell me that you have this letter until after I give you my rock bottom price first!

Ok, obviously that's fictitious (it's a reprint from a sample letter I included in my Money Magnet newsletter). Plus I personally wouldn't use price as a selling point for an artist (unless your market warrants it), but you get the idea.

One car salesman collects the name and address of everyone who comes in to check out a car. Then he sends them a personalized letter, thanking them for stopping by, and telling more about the car they looked at, its features, benefits, etc. It's still worth it even if it results in one more sale a year (and he gets more than that).

28)   Event Marketing

Ever see those plaza store events, like when a new Harry Potter book is released? All the stores get together and celebrate the launch of the book in different ways. Obviously there's the bookstore release, but the local video and game rental store gets in the act. So does the family restaurant, ice-cream vendor, and arcade. Even the dry cleaning store can get involved and pump up their business, if they stick to a common theme. And this is all announced ahead of time (with appropriate press releases, etc.) so people coming down know what to expect. "Oh, great, we can get the book for little Sally, I can drop off my suit at the cleaners, my wife can go to the apparel store. What a great time this will be for the whole family!"

29)   Start a Talk Show

If you have regular content to deliver that your target market wants, your own local talk show may be another avenue to cut through the clutter. Where I live there are plenty of local access stations that have these types of programs, and in most cases the community stations are free to air your programs. Think nobody watches them? Well, you're not going to beat out American Idol, and even infomercials will likely edge you out, but informal surveys I've conducted tell me that people are aware of these shows, and sometimes watch all or a part of one during late night channel surfing. There are even some regular "shows" that some of the locals rely on for information they can't easily get anywhere else. The key is to not do the same boring thing everyone else is doing.

In my local Rare Reminder newspaper, a local cable-access talk show host who DOES have people watching advertises for guests. If you can't start your own talk show, why not appear as a guest on one? You can get a DVD recording of it to use as a lead generation device. You can get great leads that way if your target market is watching.

30)   Know Your Customer's Lifetime Value

Yes, the "tell-a-friend" scripts are good online. The gift certificate idea mentioned previously is another. But surely there's something you can think of to really "wow" them. You want to make them say "Wait until Jane sees this!"

One of the keys to making this work (and any sort of lead generation device) is to know your customer's lifetime value. In other words, what does your average customer in this market (using the type of lead generation you are doing) bring me in profits over their entire lifetime? Let's say it's $25,000. And let's say your method of gathering leads converts 10% of leads into customers. Do you think it's wise to spend $100 per lead of that type in your efforts? Seems like a no-brainer to me.

31)   Volunteer

Besides making you feel good about helping a worthy cause, it's a great way to network if you can volunteer where you come into contact with prospects (or people who have frequent contact with your prospects).

32)   Unusual Places for Ads

I should say "unused places." Wherever a space is zoned for advertising and it's blank, there's an opportunity to get your message out. The side of a van. The side of a dumpster. Wherever.

33)   Be an In-house Speaker –

Besides getting great fees to appear and speak, you establish yourself as the expert. And like your free local mini-seminar, it's a great place to pitch your products and services.

34)   In-house Presentations

JP Maroney talked about the stadium pitch on our call. I believe he was referring to a Chet Holmes article that talked about in-house presentations and closing the sale. I'm not going to say it better than Chet, so I'll refer you to that article so you can read it yourself. Great stuff!

35) Dimensional Mail

Or "lumpy mail," as it's known is a great way to get your letter opened! They just can't resist the lumpy package. After it's opened, however, your sales letter should do its job. If you have a successful sales letter, adding a dimensional object to it will almost always bump response.

36) Get Your Online List's Home Address and Phone Number

I spoke about this on the call. One technique Gary Halbert used was to ask his list for their home address, because he wanted to send them something to help them with their marketing. Then he sent them a lumpy mail package. But he got their home address. Now he can send them direct mail pieces and cut through all the email clutter by bypassing it completely (well, actually by supplementing it). Yanik Silver mentioned this as well. He obtains their home phone number and sends them a voice broadcast (see above). Joe Vitale does this too. So does Bill Glazer. Hmm, if all of these top marketers use this technique, do you think it works?

37) Going Out of Business

If a business with the same target market as yours is going to shut down soon, why not acquire their customer list? Most brick and mortar businesses consider liquidating their inventory or equipment, but not all of them are savvy enough to sell their customer list. That could be a huge opportunity for you.

38) Alternate Franchise

You know most franchises cost big bucks to buy into. Let's say you have a profitable cleaning business that's not a franchise, with your own system for success. You can teach this system to others and sell it for much cheaper than a franchise would go for. Here's an example of a company that does just that: http://www.my-mag-uk.com. I essentially do that with entrepreneurs. I teach them my marketing system (which as you probably know most entrepreneurs don't know a lot about effective marketing), and they gain a doubled or tripled profit margin as a result.

Or, you could locate such a successful company yourself, learn their system, and teach it to others in the same manner.

39)   Office or Waiting Room Redesign

If you have an office, waiting room, or reception area for your business, get rid of all magazines and replace them with testimonials and success story books, before and after photo albums, and other publications designed to advance the sale. Replace your wall paintings with framed testimonials. Give them an avalanche of proof!

40)   Pre-paid Services

Pre-paid "memberships" have been sold successfully by many businesses, such as cosmetic surgeons, chiropractors, dental services, martial arts schools, photographers, restaurants, you name it. The idea is to offer a bundle of services or products that would cost far more if purchased separately over time than if purchased pre-paid up front.

41)   Reference USA

I mentioned this above in the "Direct Mail" topic, but it's worth its own topic. Why? Because if you have a library card, chances are you can access it for free. I don't pay the annual thousands of dollars required to access the site and compile lists of all sorts, because my local Newington library subscribes to it. My free library card gets me in for free. http://www.referenceusa.com

42) Creative Business Cards

Besides using both sides of your business cards and putting a compelling benefits-oriented message on it, there are many other creative ways to put your business card to work for you. Of course, odd-shaped and "rolodex-styled" cards stick out from the crowd as well. One real estate agent in California hands an extra three bucks and a business card to the toll collector as he crosses the bridge into San Francisco. He tells the toll collector that he wants to pay for the driver behind him, and asks him to give the driver his business card. Nine out of ten times, the driver calls, at least to say thank you. He's sold several expensive homes that way as a result.

A good lead generation device is to offer a free report or other gift on the back of the card. Then just distribute them where your prospects live.

At my local Munson's Chocolates outlet, Sales Manager Jim Florence has his business card fully imprinted with the company logo, name, phone number, and email address made out of...you guessed it...CHOCOLATE! (Best business card I've ever eaten). A relatively new technology now allows Munson's to "print" in edible ink everything from text, images, logos, and photographs. With their business cards, customers get to taste their USP. How many other businesses offer that experience?

43)   Ask Your Customers

It may sound super simple, but if you just ask your customers what they want and then give it to them, you'll be ahead of your competitors. For example, there's a local dentist who advertises on the radio that he offers a little pill that will put patients to sleep. While they snooze, he fixes years of neglect and damage in one visit. Without asking his customers, he may not have come up with this tremendous USP.

44)   Do Research to Find Out What They Want

Again, this seems like a simplistic idea, but you'd be surprised how often it's overlooked. For instance, that same dentist I just mentioned above also advertises that nobody in his office will ever lecture you about avoiding visits to a dentist or failing to care properly for your teeth. They'll cheerfully do the work that you need and that you want, without guilt or hassle. That's a powerful benefit that most patients would probably not volunteer to tell their dentists, if asked. But by researching what dental patients complain about, and why they avoid going to the dentist as often as they should, he's addressed another powerful benefit of going to see him.

45)   Positioning

Jay Conrad Levinson and Seth Godin talk about this in The Guerrilla Marketing Handbook. When Tom of Maine introduced their "all natural" toothpaste, they didn't want to directly compete with all the other toothpastes out there. So they positioned themselves as a healthy all natural alternatives. They sold it in health stores instead of supermarkets. Close-Up toothpaste used a similar tactic. Whereas most other toothpastes emphasized "no cavities" and were more family-oriented, Close-Up targeted single people and emphasized "whiteness."

An excellent book on positioning is "Positioning: The Battle for Your Mind" by Trout & Reis.

46)   Video Brochure

The same advantages a CD sales letter (above) has over a print sales letter are even greater with a video brochure. You can film your own infomercial and even if it never airs, you can distribute it on a DVD or videotape. Unlike infomercials, which have some strict guidelines, video brochures can contain practically any format. You can use the "news broadcast" format, which is restricted in infomercials. The best video brochures are those that look like television programs, since that's what people expect to see when they are watching it. Testimonials can now contain video of the person speaking. Before and after shots are great in this format as well.

47)   Data-Based Marketing

Data-based marketing can be as simple as sending a greeting card or other "touches" communications with your customers and prospects. A florist specializing in nationwide delivery of fresh orchids uses data-based marketing quite effectively. If you order a bouquet for a friend's birthday or anniversary, they note the date and occasion in their computer. Eleven months later, you'll receive a call from them, reminding you of the occasion and asking you if you'd like to send another bouquet. Restaurants do this all the time with the birthday gift certificates. Other companies take it a step further and know when their customers will need a reorder of their product. They'll send a coupon or other discount to make another sale (for example, an oil change). Nowadays with all of the "rewards" and "shopper's club cards," supermarkets and chain stores not only capture everything you purchase and when, they can send you coupons and discounts for those products you regularly purchase. Amazon sends you emails about books similar to ones you have purchased when they're released and during other promotions.

You may want to consider starting your own "rewards" type program or something similar.

48) Secret Sales

You can send your customers a postcard that has a secret discount from 10% to whatever on everything they buy in one visit. The catch is they have to come into your store to find out the amount of the discount. The chance that they may have a 75% off coupon, for example, is often irresistible to the customer.

49) Add Extra Amenities –

For physical locations, such as a car dealership, consider testing an in-house diner, barber, coffee shop, putting green, wireless internet, video arcade, playrooms for children, book stores, manicurists, climbing walls, mini-museum, ice-cream shop, etc. These can work well especially for those businesses where their customers have to wait. It may sound extravagant, but many businesses, especially those that cater to the affluent, have done this with resounding success. Why do you think McDonalds added playgrounds to most of their restaurants? Why do upscale bookstores have coffee cafés? The list goes on.

50)   Newsletters

Newsletters are a great way to keep in touch with your customers, offer them special discounts and coupons, inform them of upcoming events (a wine store can tell their customers about an upcoming wine tasting event, for example), give them recipes, articles, advice, tips on making the most of your products/services, and much more. It's a great place to slip in case studies, success stories, testimonials, and pitches for other products and services.

Here are some tips for running a successful newsletter:

- Don't make it a straight sales pitch. You want it to be something your customers look forward to receiving. Too much advertising can turn them off and equate it with junk mail. Include quality content on a variety of subjects, not all related to your business. Don't be boring.

- Keep it regular and consistent. Don't send it three times in one month and then wait 2 months before sending it out again. Quarterly is fine, but monthly is much better.

- If you have trouble coming up with regular content or don't have the time to commit to a newsletter, there are services that will do it for you. Dan Kennedy has such a service. You can also subscribe to a content service such as Pages (http://www.pagesmag.com), where they give you royalty-free articles, artwork, and much more every month.

- Proofread your newsletter. A spellchecker won't flag "four" when it should have been "fore." Tools like Microsoft Word also have grammar checkers. Check for factual accuracy and make sure dates, times, and places are all correct. Double-check coupon amounts and other numerical figures.

- Once you develop a layout that works, try to keep it consistent from issue to issue.

- Make it easy on the eyes to read. Avoid white type on black or colored backgrounds. Don't use dark blue type on a light-blue background. Use serif fonts for the body text. Don't make it look like too much work to read. Use white space liberally.

- Have a plan before you launch your newsletter. You want to have specific goals about what you want it to do for you. Should it be written in first-person from the owner? Or third person, like most newspaper articles? Do you want to have regular columns or features? Guest writers? Do your homework up front.

- Always include your contact information, perhaps even on each page.

- Feature your customers regularly. They like to see their names in print, and it's always far better to let them sell you than for you to sell yourself.

51)   Novelty Items

You can put your message on t-shirts, hats, coffee mugs, pens and pencils, mouse pads, you name it. The trick is to have a compelling image or slogan. For example, a logo or business name is boring. But a clever message or picture with a web address will get noticed more and used more.

52)   Go to the "Edge"

Seth Godin talks about this in his book Free Prize Inside. Basically, the premise is that while your competitors sell to the "middle," you find ways to sell to the edge. It sets you apart from your competition, but it's not necessarily your USP. For example, the first release of that book came packaged in a cereal box with the prominent "Free Prize Inside" displayed.

Some more examples:

- A massage salon moves their chairs outside in the summer.

- A security guard company offers its guards dressed as Beefeaters, Buckingham Palace guards, paramilitary camo-wearing high-security guards, Matrix-type outfits, or even attractive white-collar uniforms.

- A local pub built their own custom jukebox of twenty-six thousand songs in it by ripping their 1,798 CDs into a computer.

- A restaurant in Manhattan makes the average Joe's wait, but gives the VIPs an unlisted number to get to the front of the line. Strangely enough, this pleases both groups (the VIPs love to get right in, and the average folk feel special by going to an exclusive restaurant where celebrities dine and the wait is longer due to its popularity).

- Mexico has plenty of all-in-one resorts, but only one caters to overweight people.

- NakedNews.com tells the TV-style news like everyone else, but they, well, wear less.

- The Four Sisters restaurant in Myanmar doesn't bother with a check. You pay what you think the meal is worth.

- Did you ever notice how supermarkets reward their worst customers? Shoppers with the least amount of items get their own special express lane, but the poor schmuck who's buying tons of groceries (and worth much more to the store as a customer) has to endure the longest line. What if a grocery store had a special line for their best customers, staffed with extra baggers and other mechanisms to speed the checkout process?

- Commerce Bank is open seven days a week. Do you think there are people who wouldn't mind having the option to bank on Sundays? And Liberty Bank offers free ATM usage. They'll even reimburse you for fees charged by other bank's ATMs.

- A church in New York City holds an annual barbecue for fundraising. People come from miles away because if they don't, they have to wait a whole year to come again. The local German club near my house holds their German Festival every two years for precisely the same reason.

- Enterprise Rent-A-Car doesn't focus on airport rentals. But when you need a rental car for a few days while your car is in the shop, they are the first ones you call. Plus, they pick you up!

- In the instant Internet buying world, a lawn care company realized that waiting weeks for a lawn care quote was too long. By using satellite photos and public tax records, they're able to quote a cost for service before their prospects are even contacted. Now they drive down the street with a stack of Frisbees, each affixed with a sticker containing the property address and price quote, and toss each Frisbee onto the lawn.

CHAPTER 3- FREE PUBLICITY IS ALWAYS THE BEST PUBLICITY

Publicity is a great way to reach a lot of people with a limited budget. The key is to have a message that is newsworthy, which obviously changes all the time. Years ago it was enough to launch a new website. Nowadays that's too common. As I'm writing this, there's a 12-year old girl making news because of an experiment she conducted for her school's science fair: she had fast-food ice samples tested for bacteria and compared those test results with samples of toilet water from those same fast-food restaurants (about 30% of the ice samples had more bacteria in it than the toilet water).

Besides ordering your next soft drinks sans ice, this illustrates something profoundly important: news sells. You need something fresh. Something the public would want to know about.

So, that being said, let's explore some ways to get your free publicity.

53) Write a Regular Column

Whether in a newspaper, magazine, e-zine, or offline newsletter, a regular column is a great way to establish you as an expert in your field. You can also send reprints to your clients and prospects to add proof to your sales letters and promotional materials.

54) Write an Article

Articles can be anything from a short essay on a topic to a feature article in a magazine, newspaper, e-zine, newsletter, you name it. Again, article reprints help the selling job in adding proof to your persuasion.

55) Align With a Charity or Other Non-profit Organization

This is a great way to get free publicity. Let's say you've created a course on starting a mail-order business on a shoestring budget. You can hold a free seminar with local low-income families and youths, give a presentation, and then give them all free copies of the course. Be sure to issue press releases with your local newspaper, radio and television stations, and community publications. Stories like these make great humanitarian interest pieces for these media outlets. Who knows? You could be the next guest on Oprah or the Today Show!

56) Issue a Press Release

An oldie, but goodie. The trick is to make sure your press release is a newsworthy event. For example, starting a new newsletter is not necessarily a newsworthy event (but it might in certain niche markets for smaller publications). Issuing a press release about a large donation you are giving, complete with relevant background story might be newsworthy. It all depends on your target audience and the publication(s). Editors pick up press releases if they think there is news for their readers. They do not care about you or your company. Your press release must be framed that way. "What's in it for me" is very relevant here.

57)   Create a Newsworthy Event

Here's an idea that a local stereo and electronics store did that would qualify for a newsworthy press release: They arranged a "superstition obstacle course" on Friday the 13th in their parking lot, complete with ladders to walk under, a roaming black cat, mirrors to break, umbrellas to open indoors, etc.

They called all the local radio stations and invited their morning personalities to come down and take the obstacle course challenge. One radio station took them up on their offer, and broadcast lives from the event.

The result was that tons of people came down to their store to watch and take part. And of course pick up some gear or supplies while they were there. And that, of course, not only provided a boost in sales for that day, it brought in new customers and generated lots of "word of mouth" advertising for them.

Any business can do something like this; I don't care if you're a conservative lawyer or accountant. The key is to find a theme and run with it. There's no reason why a jeweler or restaurant couldn't do something like that for Valentine's Day. Or a local Irish pub could do for St. Patrick's Day. Or any retail outlet for Christmas. The list goes on and on.

58)   Attend Special Events

Watch your local news and constantly be on the lookout for events in your area where you can increase your visibility. As always, the best lead generation methods are those that introduce your products and services by way of something free (in exchange for their contact information, of course).

59)   Take Time to Get to Know Your Local Editors and Publishers

It's a lot easier to pitch a press release or idea if you already know someone on the inside. Years ago I was in the middle of writing a book, and I started shopping for an agent, figuring it was easier to go that route than to approach the publishers directly. My wife managed insurance policies at the time for a Fortune 500 company, and one of her clients was the publishing firm Simon & Schuster. One day she happened to be talking to a prominent editor, and she mentioned my book. The editor told her to have me send it to his VP, at his request. Just like that I was no longer an unsolicited submitter. It was (and to my knowledge still is) Simon & Schuster's policy to not accept unsolicited manuscripts. That contact alone allowed me to bypass that barrier.

60)   Write a Book

With Print on Demand (POD) publishers, nowadays it's easy and cheap to type up and edit a book in your favorite word processor, upload it to a POD's server, and has the book available for shipping within weeks or less. Books are also a great way to position yourself as the expert. There's something almost magical that takes place when you send your clients an autographed copy of your latest book. In their eyes, you instantly gain credibility. Your status becomes elevated. They are more likely to want to do business with you.

There's little doubt that successful people want to surround themselves with other successful people. And a book shows them that you are successful. It gives you prestige. You are now an author. It's far easier to dismiss your self-claims in a sales letter than it is from a book. The fact that anyone can have a book printed is irrelevant (at least for now).

If you don't have the time or patience to write a book, you have several options:

- You can dictate the book and have it transcribed (elance.com and guru.com are good places to get a transcript done for you, but there are many other places online and offline to have them done as well).

- You can have someone ghostwrite the book for you. Be sure to check out their previous work, though!

- You can hold a teleseminar by yourself or with other experts and have it transcribed and edited into a book.

- You can get together with other experts in your field and each contributes a chapter or two for a book.

- You can interview other experts and compile it into a book.

- You can take books that are in the public domain, update it for today, and release it as a book (you may want to consider legal resources to make sure your choice is actually in the public domain...it's not always straightforward).

As you can see, it's fairly easy to have a book done in very little time and at very little cost. Just be sure the subject and material is relevant and fills a need. Ideally a book can also be used as a selling device for a back-end item or as a lead generation device.

61)   **Blogs, Podcasts, etc.**

Yes, this is supposed to be about offline marketing methods, but in today's information age, I would be amiss if I didn't mention them.

For starters. The offline part comes in when you advertise your blog in the offline world as well (which you should).

CHAPTER 4- USING THE IDEA OF JOINT VENTURES FOR SUCCESS

Joint ventures (JVs) are one of the best ways to lure new leads and customers. By partnering with other businesses whose customers are part of your market, you have an additional profit center of incremental income. For example, an attorney can refer his clients to an accountant, and the accountant in turn refers clients to the attorney. It's a win/win situation, because many times a new business will need both an attorney and an accountant. Depending on which one they approach first (the lawyer or accountant), they'll be referred to the other.

JVs can go much further than this simple arrangement, however. They can be very complex, and there can be 3-way deals going on. In fact, JV brokers make their money by taking a slice of the profits between two or more different businesses, where he has brokered the deal and set up everything between them.

The key to making these deals work is to make sure that you let a prospective JV partner know from the start that:

- You've discovered an additional profit center for them that they are probably unaware of (offer projected profits, if possible).

- The additional profit center will not detract in any way from their current income stream.

- The additional profit center will not incur any additional costs or labor on their part to implement.

- The additional profit center will not incur any risk whatsoever on their part.

- You will perform all of the leg work to set it up.

- They can stop at any time for any reason.

There are so many potential JVs that are possible that there's no way to cover every conceivable one here. So instead I will give some examples. Some of them may be applicable to your business. Some may not. And, like the accountant and lawyer example I gave above, it's not feasible for me to cover every type of business. Therefore, you should look at each example and see how it may apply to your business. These examples are designed to get you thinking creatively. By no means is this an exhaustive list. It's designed to put you in the right mindset, where you will look at your business and others around you and see possibilities that you never noticed before.

A great course on JVs is the JV Mastery Course, by Jay Abraham and Marc Goldman. It may be out of print now, but if you can get a hold of it, I highly recommend it. If you have it, you may recognize some of these examples from the course (no need to reinvent the wheel here). Others are variations and some examples that I have personally done.

One Tip: If you try to set up a JV with a business, and they already have a deal in place with someone else, you can take that information to their competitor and say "Your biggest competitor is already doing this." And if your partner ever decides to stop the JV deal, you can go to their competitors and say the same thing (Hint: if you let them know you are going to do that, they may reconsider). Never feel that you have to partner with one specific business exclusively. Ideally you should have JV deals going on all over the place.

You can also do JVs between your business and another, or you can broker JVs between two different businesses and take a cut.

62)   Sell an Idea

A lawyer knew how to make a million dollars in a year with one person and three associates. Since many attorneys don't make that much, he codified his knowledge and had someone sell it. A realtor had a list three times better than anyone else, so she trained other realtors for a fee. A lumber mill knew how to kiln dry wood and get greater quality wood in less time with half the energy cost, saving him millions of dollars. He taught his techniques to other lumber mills. If there's something remarkable about your business, or something you know how to do better than 99% of everyone else, you have an opportunity to license or teach your skills to others.

63)   JV With Your Suppliers

Your suppliers generally want you to be more successful, since it means more sales for them. They may fund sales people, mailings, extra staff, etc. You'll never know unless you ask them.

64)   Seek Out Other Business That Cater to Your Market

I used the lawyer and accountant example above. A realtor may JV with moving companies, custom framers, carpet cleaners, pest control services, lawn care companies, painters, electricians, plumbers, the list goes on. Just be sure to JV with those businesses that have products and/or services your customers may need (i.e. a realtor JVing with a video game company doesn't make much sense).

Make a list of businesses that want and need a constant flow of leads: lawyers, doctors, dentists, realtors, home remodeling services, carpet cleaners, pest control services, etc. Broker deals between them where there is a fit to generate leads.

65)   Leverage Buyers and Sellers

A business broker sent a letter to 30,000 CPA firms saying "We've got buyers ready to pay all cash to buy your practice whether you stay or not." 500 people responded, so he took those 500 people out and mailed the other 29,500 firms saying "We've got 500 hundred firms right now that are big money makers ready to be sold. Owners will stay or not. Terms or cash is your choice." Then it was a simple matter to match the buyers to the sellers, resulting in a million dollars' worth of commissions. This is a very powerful technique that can be used in a variety of different ways.

66)   Match Front-End/Back-End Products

If you sell a high-ticket back-end product, you can seek out people who don't yet have a back-end product and JV yours via an affiliate program. Likewise, if you don't have a high-ticket back-end product, the reverse is also true. There are plenty of expensive product and service sellers out there to partner with.

You can also broker deals between businesses selling front-end books and tapes and businesses selling back-end expensive seminars, for example.

67)   JV a Sales Force

There are plenty of professional sales people that sell a variety of different products on a commission basis. It's a snap to put an ad in the paper to get these folks to sell your products and services.

68)   The Neon Sign Approach

I call this the "Neon Sign Approach" because Jay Abraham talked about a particular JV deal with a neon sign maker. He would have high school and college students drive around at night and look for neon signs that were not lit or only partially lit. Then he would pay them per "find," and report those locations to the neon sign maker. Voila! Instant leads.

A variation on this approach could be done with motor vehicles. There are numerous services to get the names and addresses from a motor vehicle registration plate. Those same high school and college students can be on the lookout for broken taillights, body damage, cracked windshields and the like. When they find one, they write down the license plate information and give it to you.

You can then supply the leads to auto repair shops, body shops, windshield replacement shops.

What if you owned a furniture store? You could JV with door-to-door salespeople and have them on the lookout for badly worn furniture. They're already going to be in their prospect's living room, right?

How about the furnace maintenance person who keeps an eye out for water damage in the basement? If you offered basement-sealing services, wouldn't you want as many furnace maintenance folks as possible getting you leads?

69)   JV Mailings

For certain product or service offerings, direct mail can be prohibitively expensive. That's why card decks and Value-Packs are so popular. But aside from those types of mailings, you can always partner with a non-competitor (or two or three) that offer a complementary or similar product/service with the same target market as yours. By splitting the cost of the mailing, you still get your message out, but at a much-reduced cost.

70)   JV Inserts/Flyers/Circulars

Similar to JV mailings, you could arrange to have your flyer, insert, or circular inserted into another publication already being mailed. This "hitching a ride" approach works best when your audience is targeted, although newspaper inserts are popular with local bricks and mortar businesses. The JV part comes into play when you pay so much per lead or a percentage of all sales resulting from the arrangement. Depending on your price structure, you can pay a percentage of the first sale only, or a tiered approach where a smaller percentage is paid for all first year purchases, a percentage of the back-end purchase, etc. You need to determine what types of deals bring in the biggest profits for you, while still providing a valuable incentive for your JV partners. And that really goes for any type of deal.

71) JV a Mini-Seminar or Teleseminar

Using the lawyer/accountant example again, the two could get together and hold a seminar for new business owners, offering a package deal for both of their services.

72) Sell Your JV

When you have an income stream from a JV deal you have worked out, you can always sell the rights to that deal to someone else. Just like a money-making website that you can sell, JVs that have a positive cash flow are assets in their own right.

73) JV Deals to Observe and Learn From a Guru

Basically, you can act as a broker or middle agent between a person with a certain expertise and others who want to learn from the expert.

74) If You're the Guru, Vice Versa

If you are the expert, the reverse is also true. You could JV with a middleman to bring people to you to pay for access to your expertise. Coaching programs are an obvious choice for this approach.

75)   JV a Dealmaker

If brokering deals isn't your forte, you can always JV with someone who sells well and knows how to negotiate to pitch and put the actual deals together for you. This way you can sit back and pull all the strings while your "agent" handles the stuff you aren't comfortable doing.

76)   Painting Fire Hydrants

One of the first deals Jay Abraham put together was paying kids to paint fire hydrants. He'd put all the deals together, the kids would go out and paint, and he'd pay them a percentage of what he was getting paid. His value was that he was the one to put it all together, he set up the deals, and he got the labor organized. This approach works well anytime there is someone willing to perform the service for less that you are getting paid.

Even 'ol Tom Sawyer did this when he had to white wash a fence in Mark Twain's Tom Sawyer. He got the local kids to do it, and they loved it.

77)   Overstock/Surplus Selling

It's not difficult to find businesses with excess inventory, tie up the rights to unload it at a discount, and then find outlets to sell it at retail. You pocket the difference. On the flip side, if you yourself have excess inventory, you could JV to find someone to unload it from you in the same fashion.

78)   JV to the Affluent

If you can partner with a business that sells a high-ticket item to the affluent, here's a blueprint worth testing:

- Choose the most popular high-ticket item they sell.

- Send a letter via FedEx to their "A" list, those 20% of customers that are responsible for 80% of their profits. Tell them about a special one-day closed door private by invite-only "showing" for that one specific product/service. Hire a professional copywriter to write a specific sales letter for that one product or service.

- Serve coffee, tea, muffins, or whatever is appropriate for that target market on the day of the showing. Make it an event, more than just the product or service itself. Look for ways to gain media exposure. Yes, it's a private showing, but if their "A' list hears about it from the media, they'll want to be there.

- Make sure they have their most knowledgeable staff on hand for the showing. You're selling to the affluent here, so you don't want to cut any corners. Find out what they want and give it, to them.

- Collect your profits, but be sure to follow-up with a thank you letter, ideally also sent to them via FedEx. And unadvertised bonuses always help!

79)   Lead Generation JVs

Find out what other businesses your target market visits. For example, I sell to entrepreneurs, and a lot of them frequent the UPS Store and other such places. FedEx/Kinkos and other "copy shops" are also ideal places where I live. Many of these places don't capture their customer's name, address, email address, etc. So I made an arrangement with them. I setup "take ones," where they can take a brochure for free, go online to my website, fax me, or mail me their contact info, then I send them a free report relevant to them. I give their contact info to the store I JV with (and

I notify the prospects of this fact...it hasn't seem to hurt my leads significantly so far). For those businesses (a Staples store, being one of them) that are stubborn, I offer to give them the contact info I collect from all the stores I JV with in their area. Again, you need to include a disclaimer when doing that, but in my tests, the benefit has outweighed the losses.

In a discussion with Michel Fortin recently, he mentioned that you need to really provide an incentive for these businesses to promote you. So the "take one" box may not be enough by itself. True, they are getting the contact info of some of their customers (something they themselves should be gathering), but if they don't know enough to get that information in the first place, they may not be as anxious to promote your free report or premium. I'm experimenting with several other ways to measure how well they will promote me, and I'll provide updates as they become available.

80) Endorsements

There are people and businesses that have a great personal relationship with their customers and prospects. They may not necessarily know this fact. In fact, a lot of them don't even realize the amount of pull they have with their audience. People who recommend certain stocks or trends, people who give great content and information to their subscribers, people who give investment advice, generally people who have a certain rapport with their subscribers. They are the ones you want to target. If their niche is non-marketing-related, so much the better in order to cut through this niche's clutter. I know someone who targeted golf enthusiasts for a marketing product, simply because of their test results. In any case, if you can JV with this sort of person who will endorse your product or service, you have a huge advantage. It's simply one of the best ways to print money on demand. Please don't overlook this technique.

These people may not even realize the relationship they have with their list. So you would be well advised to start with those folks.

81)   JV Your List Building: Large List

If you have a large list, one of the easiest ways to build it even further is to do a cross mailing. That is, you partner with another large list owner in your target market. You send out his message to your list, he sends out your message to his list. Simple. Just remember, once your prospects or customers are on another list that sells to them, there is increased message clutter. That is, they are now being pitched by your JV partner AND you. It's a tradeoff you need to consider.

82)   JV Your List-Building: Small List

Ok, if your existing list isn't large enough to warrant a cross JV mailing as described above, here's a clever way to build your list up quickly. I've done this, but not to the extent I should. I've got more deals like this in the works. Here's how it works: Let's say your list is on the small side. "John Smith" has a huge list. You want to JV with him, but a cross swap isn't going to persuade him. You need to be the middleperson between John Smith and another large list owner.

"Jane Doe" is another huge list owner. What if you can put John Smith and Jane Doe together to do a cross mailing and you get exposure as well. Instead of a cut of profits, you agree to get a slice of the list. In other words, perhaps in order to get onto Jane's list from John's, they have to come through you first. Or, you could have John mail his list with the agreement that whatever prospects Jane gets, she'll share with you. It's a win/win/win situation, because all of you are gaining new prospects on your lists.

You get some of Jane's list. Or, ideally, you get some of both lists. You are the dealmaker. It wouldn't have happened without you, so depending on the deal you make, why shouldn't you get access to both lists?

83)   JV Advertising Space

Remnant advertising is big business these days for those who how to exploit it. What is remnant advertising, aka "stand-by advertising?" A reprint from my newsletter will explain:

If you already have an effective direct mail campaign, why not tweak the same winning letter and turn it into a space ad? You already have a winning piece. You can save on costs by merely reformatting it a little to create a whole new ad. Of course, depending on your sales letter, this may or may not work. Some letters are specifically targeted for a particular niche market (as they should be). In that case, you may need to change the headline or tweak the lead, but it can usually be done for a lot less than writing a new ad from scratch. And you also gain the added advantage of speed. You can get your space ad written in this fashion a lot faster than writing from scratch. Of course, that's assuming you have the budget to take out half-page or full-page ads. What if your budget only allows for a smaller space ad?

One of the most challenging things about small space ads is trying to fit in enough copy to get the job done. "The more you tell, the more you sell" is especially true when the goal of the ad is to provoke an action from the prospect, especially an action that involves more than just picking up the phone or dropping a reply card in the mail.

So what's the most effective type of space you can use in a newspaper?

A larger one - one that gives you plenty of room to include your long and persuasive copy. If a prospect doesn't know enough about your product or service, and isn't convinced enough to act immediately, you've lost an opportunity. Repeat this to a circulation of tens or hundreds of thousands, and your ad is like flushing perfectly good money right down the toilet.

Now, there's a woman, Nancy Jones, who near single-handedly invented stand-by advertising. What is stand-by advertising? I've gotten her consent to share a letter she wrote to newspapers some twenty-odd years ago that will explain the concept: Dear Advertising Director,

Over the past several years, our client, the XYZ Company, has repeatedly expressed an interest in having his advertisements published in your newspaper.

However, our agency has compared your open rate with that of newspapers where the advertisement has already been published and we have found it necessary to advise the client against including your newspaper in his advertising schedules. This decision was based mainly on the fact the client's advertisement has been profitable only in those newspapers where a stand-by or remnant rate has been offered.

As you know, stand-by simply means a newspaper agrees to publish an advertisement whenever or wherever space becomes available and offers to reduce the open line rate to the advertiser for "standing by." Space may become available due to last minute cancellations of scheduled advertisements or because of production difficulties. Whatever the reason, the newspaper will generally insert a house ad or a public service ad to fill the hole in the newspaper. Therefore, more often than not, the newspaper receives no revenue for the use of this space.

Thus, stand-by advertising has become advantageous for both the newspaper and the advertiser. The newspaper has the opportunity to make money on space it might otherwise have to give away. The advertiser is able to use a publication it could not use at the open rate.

More and more newspapers are becoming involved in stand-by advertising. Enclosed is a current list of newspapers offering a stand-by program and the discounts they allow. We are aware your newspaper has not offered a stand-by rate in the past but we would like very much for you to consider this possibility now. We are enclosing an insertion order for a full page, a mechanical and a check for the new amount of the order. The net amount has been computed at the open rate discounted by 50% for stand-by, normal for the industry, and 15% for the standard agency discount.

If you accept our offer, simply hold the material until space becomes available. If and when the opportunity presents itself, run the ad, cash the check and send us a tear sheet. If you do not wish to participate at this time, simply return the check to the agency and destroy the mechanical.

This offer expires in 15 days. Please feel free to call if you have any questions about the offer or our client.

Sincerely,

Nancy Jones

The newspaper just can't resist the fact that they have a check in hand, more profits for them, for utilizing advertising space that would have otherwise yielded zero dollars in revenue.

Jeff Collins

In a recent telephone call with Nancy, she told me that advertisers typically pay 3 times the amount for a 4-inch by 4-inch ad than she can get for a quarter-page ad. She has such purchasing power now that she can get ads at around 10% the normal going rate! And that includes her fees. That means with stand-by advertising, you can get the same size ad as your competitors for one-tenth the cost! I hope your mind is spinning with the possibilities here. You can reach Nancy at 727-535-7899

It includes her letter above, plus a lot of useful information from Gary. I won't repeat what Gary says about positioning your ad, or any of the great advice he gives, so head on over to read it all.

By the way, if you haven't heard of Gary, he's one of the best marketers and copywriters in the world. I highly recommend reading all his newsletters if you don't already. There are more proven marketing ideas in his newsletters than there are leaves on a tree, so get on over there and start reading. WARNING: If you're like me, you'll have trouble sleeping after reading it, because your mind will be racing with ideas!

So how can this benefit a JV enthusiast? Well, what do you think Nancy Jones is doing? She's doing deals with newspapers around the country and offering reduced advertising costs to her clients. If you're a marketing consultant, do you think Nancy can help you and your clients? Is it possible to make your own deals with newspapers, magazines, and other publications? You betcha! Jay Conrad Levinson even talks a great deal about this in his Guerilla Marketing books. You merely need to move beyond concept into ACTION!

84)   Rekindle Procrastinating Customers

Here's something you can do for your own business, or you can do a JV with another business and capture some of the "found" revenue. Many customers tend to procrastinate on their purchases. For example, a dentist may have 3000 patients, but after analysis, 1000 haven't come back in over a year. A sequence of mailings to these 1000 (with incentives to come back) might bring back a certain percentage, of which you can negotiate up front a slice of the profits.

This may be nothing new to you. But most dentists know about dentistry, not marketing. How about the carpet salesman who has customers that haven't replaced their carpets in six years? If the average customer replaces his carpet every five years, you have an opportunity to offer them an incentive to act now.

85)   Rekindle Former Customers

In addition to customers that procrastinate, there will always be customers, for one reason or another, that no longer purchase from a business. Perhaps they've moved out of the area. They may no longer have a need for your product/service (i.e. baby clothes...the baby eventually grows up). They may have passed away. There are lots of reasons why. And then there are those customers who are dissatisfied.

You want to target most of them. For those that are dissatisfied, you want to offer them an opportunity to make things right, to give them a special deal if they agree to give you another try. For the others, they are most likely satisfied former customers. For whatever reason, though, they are no longer part of the target market. The best way to capitalize on that situation is to get them to refer business to you. If they are satisfied, they may respond

Jeff Collins

favorably to a gift certificate that they can pass onto a friend or relative who IS still part of the target market.

Either way, it's "found" business, and you stand to profit from it.

Let's say you want to target chiropractors. You can locate a bunch of authors who are reputable and recognized by chiropractors, contact them, and tell them what you're doing. Ask to buy a bunch of copies of their book at a discount if they would be willing to send a letter to these chiropractors along with their book (at your expense). The letter would say something like, "Hi, this is John Smith here. You probably know me through my book, '17 Ways to Grow Your Chiropractor Business Today.' It's been reviewed in Health Economics, and I'm sending you a copy of my book with my compliments and introducing you to Jane Doe, because she's got a great way to reactivate your no longer active patients. I've asked her to email you in about a week."

86)   JV With an Agent to Bring in "Found" Business

If you want to focus on your core business, like the dentist example I mentioned about (i.e. let's say that you're the dentist), and you're not sure how to go about bringing in this "found" business, there are experienced marketers out there who could handle the nuts and bolts of the campaign. In other words, this would be the reverse of the previous two examples, where you are the professional, and a deal with a marketer would yield you additional business, but without the marketing headaches. At the very least you could pay someone to teach you how it's done, or learn by example in observing their methods and asking questions.

87)   JV a Consulting Back-End With a Static Product Seller

Let's say that you are a consultant specializing in doing creative real estate deals. You could find someone who sells a static book or course on the subject, then partner with them to offer your coaching or consulting services on the back-end for those that want to go beyond the book or course. You could offer your own course, seminars, and coaching programs, whatever.

88)   JV a Static Product with a Consulting Back-End and the opposite is also true.

If you sell a static information product, why not seek out an expert on the subject that you can partner with and endorse for additional training for your customers. Everybody wins!

89)   Tie Up the Rights to Real Estate

I don't mean real estate in the traditional sense. I mean space. Using the chiropractor example, what if you opened a satellite office that's manned once or twice a week in a health club or health food store? You could put lots of things in those places. Acupuncture, Shiatsu, massage therapy, weight-loss clinics, exercise products, the list goes on.

Instead of an office, you could tie up the rights to a display space or an impulse buy counter near the register. How about a segment of the store, the rear section of a store, or the front corner where merchandise or services can be placed? Banks now put branches in grocery stores. So do flower shops. Sears put Allstate Insurance in their stores and created a billion dollar business. Designer shampoos have space in salons.

If you tie up the space first, then you can go out and find inventory that you will in essence consign to the space. Anywhere there is foot traffic is really fair game. Just be sure to find a product or service that is a match to the foot traffic's preferences (i.e. the target market). There is lots of one or two-person companies who manufacture their own jewelry, or candy, or cookies, or toys, or crafts. Maybe a local hotdog joint doesn't have cookies on their menu. Put them together and take a cut. How about craft supplies and raw materials at a craft show? A service in a hotel that perhaps that hotel doesn't offer? Maybe free wireless Internet access in exchange for their contact info. The nice thing is you don't have to put up any inventory.

Vacant lots are great to put in cars for sale. You can also organize your own flea market or craft show or a haunted house around Halloween, sponsored by the local costume shop. A golfing goods tent that coincides with the timing of the US Open is yet another good idea.

I've mentioned some of these ideas already, but this example is about tying up the rights to space. Get the rights first, then looks for ways to fill it.

90) JV With Those Who Already Have Business Relationships

I mentioned at the start of this section that some of the best companies to JV with are those whom you already have a preexisting relationship with. What if you don't have any?

You can JV with those people who do! Put an ad in your local paper. Go online and network with people who do have these relationships. Then cut them in on the deal and let them introduce you. It's the difference between a cold intro and a warm or hot one.

91)   Start Small

Do you have a big idea for a deal but no relationship with the potential partner company? You can always start out small, with a test to validate your experience and the results before moving onto the big deal you had in mind. By the time your small deal is validated, you know have that relationship to move to the next level.

92)   Let Them White Label You

Let's assume you are an IT consulting firm, and you decide to JV with hardware companies to access their customer base and have them endorse your services. The trouble is, you want to JV with several hardware makers, and each one wants you to use only their hardware. How do you get around that and still have access to all of their lists and endorsements?

One way is to let them "white label" your services. In other words, when you consult for their customers, you represent that hardware company. So every time you go out, you change "shirts and hats," so to speak. That way each hardware company has you representing them. Basically, they would sell your services as their own.

Think of it as a "private label rights" situation, where you sell your works to other companies that they can in turn repackage as their own. If you're looking to drum up more business, this one approach alone could bring you more than you can handle. In other words, you may have to hire more staff. It's that powerful.

Listen, do you think all of the "Geek Squads" and such are all owned by the companies dispatching them? No, many are contracted. These are large-scale corporate deals, but nothing says you can't do something similar on a smaller scale to start.

93)   JV the Costs

Whether it's an office you share, or a receptionist, or an administrative assistant, or standby conference call lines, you can make deals with other businesses that may not need a full-time receptionist, for example, to keep the costs down. A local school supply business shares an office with a surveyor. A small downtown Hartford mail order firm shares office space and conference rooms with an advertising agency. A New York investment consulting firm shares the mailing address with a Florida realtor who is also licensed in New York and wants a local presence. Things like office and mail services help desk support, and other shared services are becoming more common. If you can't find one that makes sense for your business, why not invent your own solution?

94)   JV to Build Your List

Your list is your greatest asset, right? But if you only have 1,000 names where 50,000 or 100,000 is the norm (more is better, right?), then why not JV a list exchange. Bear with me. It's true that you may not have much to offer to the list owner of 100,000+ names, when you only have 1,000. But it can be done.

One way to do this? Ok, let's pretend that I convince a speaker to do a teleseminar with me that I know at least 2 or 3 other 100k+ list size owners would love to tell their subscribers about. Let's couple that with the fact that these list owners want to build their lists even more. And you do too. You could make a deal with some of these list owners that whoever opts in to your teleseminar, you'll do a solo mailing of a product of their choice to the entire list if they promote the call. Remember they're delivering a message to their list that their list would be interested in, and they're interested in getting the names of the other list owners that will opt-in. So you act as the middle-person and make all sides happy, while greatly adding to the size of your list.

I've personally done this, and I've got some big promotions on the way that will grow my list even further. All you need to do is to contact these people and let them know how they benefit from the arrangement.

Will everyone welcome the deal? No. But there are plenty who will. And everyone wins (those are the best kinds of deals, by the way). This is one of those ideas that will work just as good online as they do offline.

95)   School Deals

You can contact local community colleges and other educational learning institutes and offer to teach a course for free or for a salary. While you'll teach them valuable skills, the logical outcome of your course is for them to purchase your full-course and other information products. While I haven't personally done this, I know of others who have, and it's a great way to both establish you as an expert and make money on the back-end as well. And the inevitable publicity doesn't hurt, either.

96)   Company Speeches/Seminars

Lots of companies give in-house speeches and seminars. Most charge a nominal sum. You can do the same, and sell your products and services. It's a great way to get into a company and do your pitch.

97)   Friends and Relatives

One of the best ways to get started in JV deal making is by working with people you already know well and who trust you. I'm talking about friends and relatives who are entrepreneurs. Look, there's a reason why MLM companies like Tupperware and the Pampered Chef do so well. Most of their first-time salespeople sell to their friends and relatives first. My younger brother sold a set of knives to my mother that she still uses to this day (after years). I used to sell Mason Shoes door to door when I was a teenager (yes, admittedly a LONG time ago). Guess who my first buyers were?

Well, the same thing works for JVs. I have some friends who opened up a restaurant. I'm now working with them, without any money out of their pocket, to develop JV deals that will build additional profit centers for them. And yes, I get a cut. When you work with folks that are close to you, you tend to have their vested interest at heart. And that sets the stage for JV deals with "cold" prospects, because you also want to be known as having their best interests at heart.

You are the dealmaker. You make it happen and know all of the ins and outs of business. This comes with time, so the more deals you make (even the unprofitable ones), the better you'll be equipped to handle the bigger more profitable ones.

98)   JV Anything You Need

Need a room to hold your seminar? A rental car? Your hotel or airfare covered? Any expense, rental, or use of a product or service? Why not use your product or service to JV what you need. Michel Fortin used to do this with a local hotel. He would get the room for free and hold all of his seminars there, getting new leads and business. While his seminar attendees were there, they used the hotel's business center, giving the hotel business as well. It was a win/win situation.

JP Maroney worked out a deal to get his room for free to hold his mini-seminar as well. Jay Abraham regularly did deals to get cars, airfare, you name it.

99)   JV for Airtime

Yes, it's even possible to JV with radio and television stations for free airtime for your ads and infomercials. Every radio or television station has some unsold airtime. They have to use it for something. They only need to fill a certain amount of public service time. After that, the rest of the time is used for the most profitable way they can come up with. If you present a compelling offer to them, yours may be more desirable to them. Simply find out what they want, and offer it to them for an exchange of airtime.

NOTE: This technique is done more often than you think, mostly by ad agencies and bigger companies. But even with that going against you, there is still a considerable amount of unsold time available, especially in the smaller stations. Hint: You don't have to do the deal with only one station at a time.

100)   Leverage JV with Bartering

This is another little-known technique you can use to make your deals even more lucrative.

Let's say that you found out that your local radio station WXXX needs a new roof. So you do a deal with the local roofing company J&J Roofing, where you trade your services for a roofing job. J&J charges $10,000 for a new roof needed by WXXX. But it only costs them $3,000 in labor and materials. The other $7,000 is profit. So you provide $3,000 worth of services to J&J, get $3,000 worth of labor and materials in result, and are able to give WXXX a new $10,000 roof for only $3,000 worth of services. Now you get J&J's $7,000 profit.

Listen, it does work that way more often than you think. Jewelry, cars, furniture, services, and just about anything you can think of that were produced by a for-profit company always has that kind of leverage if you work the deal the right way.

101)   "Think Outside the Box"

Yes, I know it's a cliché. But in this case, it's very true and profitable. The examples I provided here aren't by a long shot every possible technique you can use. Rather, they are designed to get you thinking in the proper "mindset." You'll soon see that there are more possibilities and opportunities around you that you may have not noticed before. So your job is to always be on the lookout for them. And recognize them when they do catch your attention. Will they always be profitable? Hardly. But as you get more and more exposed to this kind of creative marketing thinking, you'll be better equipped to spot the ones that are more frequently up front.

The best advice I can give you to that end is to try some of these ideas for yourself. Make them your own. Find out what works best for your business and which ones don't. Read more than one newspaper each day. Read trade journals and magazines. Read what your target market reads. There's opportunity everywhere if you know where to look.

CHAPTER 5- SHOULD YOU TRUST MARKETING GURUS?

Most marketers are lost in the fog of information overload. Because of this, they eventually are lured by a guru claiming to have all the answers to their marketing woes. The guru also promises you can make a fortune by just following their advice. Of course that advice comes with a hefty price tag. So what is the truth? It is a land of smoke and mirrors, a carnival of lies that is directed at you for the sole purpose of taking your money don't kid yourself here.

Most gurus want to turn you into their affiliate machine, recurring ATM and use you for their traffic regardless of what most promise to teach you. Some gurus are actually setting you up to fail! They know that the more you fail, the more you will spend out of sheer frustration. You will be given just enough information to get your interest up and then you will be asked to spend more money on the latest shiny fad the guru has. Yet the real truth is that many of these gurus laugh at you as being too stupid to know any better.

The same is true of most of the "free traffic generation" gurus. The gurus love the traffic niche as it appeals to almost everybody who wants to make a living online. Incidentally, people who do not understand how to generate traffic are usually clueless about marketing strategies.

Newbie's are the guru's favorite target. Some of these gurus were well intentioned (at one point) and had great ideas for building traffic but they learned it was just easier to resell crappy traffic, almost worthless programs for making traffic and marketing courses for unsuspecting folks for easy money.

Getting the Most from Guru Services

1. Traffic Exchanges

If you ever wanted to be a hamster on a wheel then feel free to join one of the many traffic exchanges that exist online. What amazes me is that many people still love traffic exchanges despite the fact that very little of their traffic ever converts into anything of value.

Exchanges look flashy, colorful and it always appears like there is a whole lot going on from a marketing perspective that can benefit you. I have seen people devoting hours each day "clicking" like mad to earn credits and what is equally ridiculous about this is that on the other side of the computer are equally desperate marketers clicking as fast as they can to do the same.

Many of the top exchanges even have incorporated a social aspect and other related MLM like services to keep you interested and yes, clicking like crazy; or investing your money to sell your site views to others who are frantically clicking.

The problem is, nobody is actually looking at anyone else's offers and the truth is these services are only great if you own the traffic exchange. While traffic exchanges can and do send traffic to your site(s) most people discredit the psychology behind what makes traffic exchanges tick. People believe that they are getting good quality traffic and earning visits by clicking and visiting other sites; yet most people are clicking like mad and never stop look or engage any of the ads / sites that are displayed because there is no incentive to do so!

The few marketers that understand this make sure their site immediately grabs the attention of visitors because you have just a few seconds to say something that will break the "clicking trance" most people are under.

Traffic exchanges work well by taking advantage of newbie's. They are duped to buying traffic, signing up to lots of offers and eventually they come to the realization that nobody cares about their site(s)! Why? People will leave as soon as the timer allows them to (clicks are timer driven so you must stay on the current site for at least a few seconds, but the name of the game is to rack up lots of credits, so that is what people do).

If you doubt this give it a try and look at your logs for traffic stats and see how long the typical visitor from a traffic exchange stays on your site. I guarantee you, 99% of the time; it's no longer than the timer on the exchange.

How to Get the Most Value from Traffic Exchange

Anyone who has been on a traffic exchange for any length of time eventually figures out that this kind of traffic usually does not work to converting buyers, at least not directly. Most marketers use splash or squeeze pages and offer something to try to entice people to opt in to their offer. Where is the real gold? Additional traffic offers! Think about it.

Why are people on the exchange in the first place? They want traffic to their sites. So what is a good way to work the traffic sites? Make a page that promotes the exchanges with your referral id. Here is a good example of leveraging multiple sites and rankings (cleverly disguised) this has referral IDs in each of the major traffic exchanges in it. Since most people in a traffic exchange are curious about other ones, this works well to drive sign ups and eventually make you money and more traffic credits.

You can run this page on multiple sites as well and benefit from the people looking for more traffic exchanges. Bottom line: if you love traffic exchanges then find a way to sell traffic, refer other exchanges or just buy your own traffic exchange. At least you will have a captive audience to market your clicks and other related offers to. This is the real and only reason traffic exchanges exist regardless of the crap you are told.

2.Ad Swaps, Solo Ads and Mailing Lists

Many people have discovered they can build a business selling ads in the form of mailings if they have a good size list to offer. At first glance, this seems to be a great way to build traffic; pay a little money get a guru to do a mailing for you to their list. You can make money selling your products and even grow your own mailing list at the same time. Brilliant! While this is very possible, beware.

Here are the caveats:

Scam #1 Freebie Lists

You will probably see clicks and signups but many of these scammers build huge lists of freebie seekers (lowest class of marketing segment) and then resell these "Solo Ads" to people. They promise so many open clicks for your email and usually you can get some sign ups too. The problem is that the real value is to a marketer's BUYER list. It is easy to get freebie seekers to sign up but many of these people will not buy anything.

Scam #2 –All Signups from One Place

Be careful with deals from overseas areas. You will get sign ups to your offer but they are all seem to be from one place! More than likely the people you just signed up are sitting in "overseas sweat shops" and are paid a few pennies every time they join a list or do something related to this.

Be very careful! Be wary of overseas list sharing or paid ads and if you see signups coming all from one IP address or geographical location, odds are you have been had and never do business with these people again. This has become big business and unsuspecting marketers, even the big names, fall for this scam all the time!

The scammers are getting better with this scam as they are using software that rotates their IP's or multiple proxies to cover their tracks. If you do decide to try this make sure you do your homework on who is selling / swapping a list to. Look for reviews and reputable places where other marketers have reported on the success of the list they ran their ad with. Good marketers will make this information available if they are selling ads. If you get a reputable ad swap or buy keep in mind that you should consider removing the double opt in.

I realize some people will say this is a risk when it comes to the spam laws but the double opt in will greatly reduce your sign ups during the ad run. Also make sure your offer for your mailing list is a really GOOD offer. It should be a good product or service that has real value.

Another factor to watch is your opt outs. If you get sign ups then a few days or week later you get a bunch of un-subscribers, either your offer sucks or again you have been taken to the cleaners. I suggest a site called Safe Swaps that is policed by its members and is a paid list building service so there is at least a barrier to entry, (scammers do NOT want scrutiny) a history of swaps and their effectiveness as well as a way to suss out scams.

3. Blast It Ads, FFA's And Your Ad to Millions

You are told for a fee (or your email) you can blast an ad to millions of places that will explode your traffic, sales and help your lists grow. What you are not told is that these free for all sites (called FFAs) simply place your ad on some buried low value website page by a bot and your ad will never be seen by anyone. Sure your ad will be either sent to or posted to millions of these kinds of sites – yet if no human ever sees these ads . . . What good are they?

People set up these kinds of sites for one reason; to be able to send you spam! When you sign up to have your ad posted you agree to receive email notifications about your ad status, which seems reasonable. Marketers will send you repeated confirmations about your ad (your ad is live, your ad is now on page 5 please bump it up back to page 1, your ad is no longer showing please refresh your ad) and of course promote all kinds of crap to you in the process with riders on the emails they send you.

You can expect oceans of spam mail and remember most of these ads eventually roll off these sites so you will need to re post over and over. Still what is the use? If only bots (and maybe you) see your ad what good is it? FFA's (free for all sites) have no value to you unless you own one and turn the tables on these gurus. Free viral traffic most are unworkable or just feed your emails to a list that someone will try to sell you crap – and of course you will be stuck promoting other people's product(s) first before you see any real traffic or forced to "upgrade" to the paid version to make it work. I have seen this variation in all kinds of marketing. In general you are told your URL will go viral and you add your website to a list of says 5 other people who have done the same.

Now go somewhere and send this to some people and they will do the same causing your ad / url to be seen by millions . . . This seems probable and the math makes sense; but the real issue here is human nature – the focus of this tool is supposed to be to get people to look at your site. The problem is just like the traffic exchange, or FFA page issue; nobody cares about you or your business unless you give them a really good reason to do so and they only care about their success, thus there is no motivation to seriously consider visiting your site and using your offer!

So again this fails miserably as people are only concerned with themselves and do not care about your success. The best viral traffic offers that seem to have some promise always include a what's in it for me aspect but it is the originator of this program that gets the real traffic benefit not the people who add their link and push this to other people. Again you need to be the creator of a viral traffic idea and make part of this page dedicated to something you know these people can benefit immediately from or this will not work.

4. Traffic Getting Software

Almost daily there are the latest "secret release" about how some dude struck it rich because they uncovered the latest "plugin" or freak algorithmic discovery software, or how some underground internet marketer from Russia broke the traffic code . . . that allows you to hack the internet and drive tons of traffic to your website with the push of a button.

In 15 years of marketing products online I have never seen anything software based that works like these ridiculous claims say. The ads these gurus run make this stuff sound cool and sleek and how fortunate you are to have found this software and how this can't stay on the market long to protect the product so you had better sign up or else miss out.

Don't be fooled! I guarantee you it is pure bullshit. If you take the time to do your homework you will discover that these kinds of scams set up shop, rip people off and vanish. I have seen this scam done so many times it really shocking to me how many people fall for this.

Nine times out of ten the software they push is some rip-off of free or shareware with a few tweaks a programmer was paid to make from ODesk for 50 bucks and will never work as shown. NO software can generate the kind of traffic you need, not without a human component. Sorry. It's just a fact at least at the moment.

There are legitimate software offers that can help you generate traffic, but nine times out of ten you can only partially automate the process. Perhaps someday there really will be a "magic bullet" software but don't bet on it.

5. Guaranteed Traffic

It has been my experience that almost all "guaranteed traffic" sites are little more than frauds. You pay money and they deliver supposedly high quality traffic and you just sit back and make money. Yeah right.

Here are some of the ways they rip you off;

1. Pop under's that are annoyances and are usually blocked (and hardly visible if they are not) and people click off immediately (but counted as legitimate traffic to you by these places)

2. Bots visiting your site every few minutes (no human) until your "traffic" is delivered and your hit counter or analytics record it

3. Overseas sweat shops that sell clicks (dozens of people sitting in a room in China clicking on ads that have no intention or even the money to buy anything from you even if they wanted to)

These can be easy to spot as you will see traffic all from the same IP address. More complex scams have software that rotates their proxies and IP addresses. Spotting them also works by having a look at your weblogs. Your average visitor will stay at the page for some time before closing it. So have a look at your logs and see how long people are staying.

Take your average user and weigh that against some of the more suspicious ones. Keep in mind that bots such as Google or Yahoo will identify themselves very clearly in your logs and might have a short visit period.

Jeff Collins

The unique visitor that stays say 5 seconds and seems to stay only 5 seconds visit after visit is most likely part of a scam. NEVER pay for traffic except possibly for legitimate and proven media buys or other reliable tried and true sources.

CHAPTER 6- ONLINE MARKETING TACTICS NOT EVERYONE KNOWS

- Foursquare Marketing

Foursquare is an app for smartphones and android phones that allows people to check in when they visit certain local businesses.

Many business owners haven't yet to hear about Foursquare, while others have been on it since it launched back in 2009.

Why Businesses Are Not Using It

The two biggest factors that are holding small business owners back from using Foursquare are:

a. That they don't even know about it.

b. They think that it's an app to be used by customers only.

For this latter obstacle, it is sort of true. Foursquare is an app for smartphones and android phones that allows customers to "check in" when they have reached a certain location.

So if you're the owner of Debbie's Little Baby Boutique, you can add your location to Foursquare and then when customers come to see you at your store, they can check in that they are there. This spreads the word about your business and, could even bring more people in through the door.

Say you're not the owner of the Little Baby Boutique, but of Debbie's Pub. When people check in that they are there, their friends can see that and can come to enjoy a cocktail with them.

They check in, their friends see they're there, and even more people come to congregate and spend time with their friends. Already, just from that one initial check-in, you've taken a $20 tab and increased it to $100.

The profits to be realized are obvious – and there are a lot of them.

If you don't know about Foursquare and your business isn't on it, you're losing all of those potential profits.

The second biggest problem that small business owners face when considering using Foursquare for their business is that they think it's for customers only.

This is partially true, as it will be mostly customers that will be checking in when they arrive at your business.

But when you think about it, the product or service you're selling is also mainly for the customer; yet it's still something that has a huge benefit for you because that's how you make your profits. The same is somewhat true for Foursquare.

Even though customers will be the main ones to use it – they're definitely not the only ones. There are tons of ways that you can use Foursquare for your business, and you can even check into your own business every day, thereby once again telling people where you are and spreading the word about your business.

How to Use Foursquare

To begin using Foursquare you only need a few things.

You will need:

• A smartphone or an Android phone

• The Foursquare app

• A Twitter or Facebook account.

First, your smartphone and Android phones will be your link to Foursquare, and so you need to know how to get the app on your phone.

Below are the three most common types of phones, with the corresponding links and instructions for downloading the app.

For the BlackBerry

You can visit the App World right from your phone, search for Foursquare, and then download it onto your phone. If you don't want to download it from your phone, either because your phone isn't handy at the moment or because you simply prefer downloading straight from the Internet, you can visit the App World and use the link to download the app.

For the iPhone, iPod, or iPad

Downloading the app for your Apple device is just like downloading it for the BlackBerry, except that you'll be using a different link. Again, either just opens up the App Store on your device, search for it and download it.

For the Nokia

Downloading the app on your Nokia is a bit more complicated than downloading it for either the BlackBerry or Apple devices, only because you first need to make sure that the app is compatible with the type of phone you have.

Luckily, checking your compatibility is easy. Visit the Nokia website and click on "Nokia phone selector." The website will pull up a list of the phones they offer, and all you have to do is click on the model of phone you have. Once you do and find out that your phone Is compatible, the website will give you step-by-step instructions for downloading the app to your phone.

For an Android phone:

Even though there is no one website or App Store that you can visit to download Foursquare for your phone, you can still access it. Visit the Google Play and it will pull up what devices you have, as well as give you instructions on how to download it.

What If You Want to Use It To Market Your Business?

Using Foursquare isn't difficult, and setting up your page will take mere minutes.

Maintaining and managing it yourself on the other hand, is something else altogether.

And, there is more to Foursquare than just setting up a page.

This section of the guide will walk you through, step by step, how to set up Foursquare for your business, and how to manage and maintain it so that you can use it most effectively and efficiently for marketing your business.

Creating a Page on Foursquare

Before you create your page on Foursquare, you must first to see if it's already listed. Someone could have already visited your business and added it to let other people know that they are there. If you find your business is listed already, you can't just leave it; you have to then claim it. After you've claimed the page as your own, you can just start using it to boost your business. You will not have to worry about adding the page yourself; but you will need to learn to utilize it to best profit your business. That will be covered in a separate section.

If your business hasn't yet been added, you'll need to create your page. And to do that, you'll first need to sign up for an account.

To sign up for Foursquare, you'll be asked some very basic information, and you'll be asked to supply a profile photo. The photo is not a requirement, but considering that everything online is so visual today, it's only good business sense to include one.

Once you've searched for your business and signed up for Foursquare, you then need to create a page for your business on Foursquare (if one is not already on there.) Then you'll need to choose whether you want to decide if you want to connect to Foursquare through Facebook or Twitter.

Once you're all signed up on Foursquare, either through Facebook or Twitter, you're ready to continue on with creating your Foursquare page.

Once you've chosen how you want to sign into Foursquare (Twitter or Facebook) you'll be automatically redirected to the "Page Settings" page, where you can complete your page. This will involve uploading a picture that will be your profile picture to be used on Foursquare.

You can also include any banner images that you can use to promote your business, along with a description of your business and any links that will lead visitors to your other locations.

The last thing you'll need to do in the "Page Settings" page is link the Foursquare account to your Facebook account. This is different than signing in with Facebook, because this step will post anything you post on Foursquare to your Facebook account.

So how do you link your Foursquare page to Facebook?

Linking to your Facebook page from Foursquare is easy. Scroll with your mouse over top of your name in the top right-hand corner of any page on Foursquare. This will pull up the "Settings" option, which you should click on. This will give you the option "Sharing with other networks" and then click on "Add Facebook." It's here that you'll also be able to "Add Twitter" – and you should do both!

Top Marketing Tactics That Boost Sales

When you link to your Facebook, you'll need to authenticate your Facebook page, after which you'll be redirected back to your Foursquare page.

Here you'll be asked which Facebook page you want to link to, and then just click "Link." Now all of your shouts will also be pushed to your Facebook page.

Managing your Foursquare Page

The management of your Foursquare page will be the area that you find takes the most time, and you need to constantly stay on top of it so that your Foursquare page is always current and always has fresh new content.

And of course, so that you can always use all the tips and tricks to promote your Foursquare page (those will be covered later on in this guide.)

First, let's get started learning how to manage your page.

Log into your Foursquare account with the same login information that you used to verify yourself as manager. Once into your account, scroll over to the top right-hand corner of your screen and find the drop-down menu.

From here you can choose the "Page Management" option. If you have more than one page on Foursquare you'll need to choose the page that you want to work on. Then click on "Act As," which will also be found on the right-hand side of the dialogue box. This will redirect you back to your page. While you are acting as your business' page, a yellow navigation bar will appear at the top to tell you that you're working as your business.

Every action you take while you're acting as your page will show up as your page doing that action. This means that if you check into a business while acting as your own business, it will look as though your own business was there.

The first actual management task that you should do is leave tips for other venues.

Just like commenting on other business' blogs and websites this leaves your name on yet another website, and every person that visits that venue on Foursquare and sees your business' name might just check out your venue too.

Find businesses that you've actually visited and that you have helpful information to give to other people.

Is there a zoo in your area that you've visited? Give a tip on which exhibit is best to see first.

Have you been without a seat at your local theater because you arrived too late? Leave a tip on their page telling other people to get there with plenty of time before the show starts.

This not only promotes your own business but also lets others know that you're not only on the network to promote your own business – something they'll appreciate. Adding a tip is easy. At the top of any page in Foursquare you'll see the "Page Management" link. Then just choose the page you want to add tips for, and then leave whatever tip you want!

Along the same line, encourage users to leave tips for your business, too.

Top Marketing Tactics That Boost Sales

You may know everything about your business, but you still never get to see it from a customer's perspective and they could have some very valuable insights to your business, and what's best for the customers.

Maybe there's a certain staff member that customers like to deal with and they want to tell others; or maybe there's a certain spot that's the best place to sit in your café. These are things that might not be known to you, but they might be felt by every customer that comes into your business. These are tips that are helpful to others, and to your business.

The next step that you'll have to take is to add friends.

Remember, even though Foursquare might be a social network that is localized and focuses on promoting businesses and telling people about them, it's still a social network.

This means that you still need to add friends and try to build your network as large as you can. To do this, make sure to add everyone that's in your Gmail contacts, as well as your Facebook friends and your Twitter followers. Don't worry about it too much if you don't have a lot of friends at first. Even though it's been around for years, Foursquare is still very new to many people so you might not have a huge long list at first. And because Foursquare is such a localized network, you might only want to add people who are close to your physical location. This is a decision you'll need to make for yourself, as this won't be the most profitable strategy for every business.

Next, you have to get active on the network.

This involves checking in with your own business every day that you go to work.

This has several benefits for the business owner.

The first is that it tells people where you work, in case they want to come visit you while you're there (and they might just buy something when they do.)

The second benefit is that it's a continuous reminder to people that your business is out there, just waiting to serve them!

And the third is that it will help you become "Mayor" of your business. What is that, and why is it important?

In addition to being a social network, Foursquare is also a game.

In fact, it started out as a game and quickly grew into the buzzing social network it is today. Every time a person checks into a location, they earn points and a certain number of points will earn them badges – and you too! Be the one who checks into a certain business the most, and you'll become Mayor of it! And who else should be Mayor of your town but you?

- **Mobile Website**

According to Wikipedia, it is described as "the use of browser-based Internet services, from a handheld mobile device, such as a smartphone, a feature phone, or a tablet computer, connected to a mobile network or other wireless network."

In short, a mobile website is an app that allows online websites to be viewed on mobile devices – anytime, anywhere.

Having a mobile website isn't just a good suggestion for business owners today; it's a must unless your goal is to lose customers by the day. Nearly all business owners have realized by this point just how important the Internet is to their business – and many have already gone to great lengths to promote the blogs on their website, take full advantage of SEO opportunities, and in many cases even build a full e-commerce website.

But while that main website is definitely a huge source of revenue, there's another website that you could be missing, and that could be even more important than your main website.

Creating their very own mobile website is an intimidating thing to many business owners, because they think that they'll need an extensive knowledge of HTML coding and programming know-how. That may be true, depending on the type of mobile website that you're looking to create for your users and how original you'd like your mobile website to be.

But no matter how complicated, or how basic, you want to make it, this report is the guide that will show you how.

Here you'll find everything from the biggest challenges you'll face, how to overcome them, a breakdown of the different options that are available, and the easiest way to get those options.

Internet consumers don't care whether you're a techie genius or try to avoid computers at all costs. They want an online shopping experience that they can get to no matter where they are, and what device they're using to get there.

What Makes a Mobile Website Challenging?

Everything has its own challenges; and it would be unfair to say that building a mobile website is without its own. If you're a business owner and you don't already have your mobile website up and running, you may already be facing some of these challenges –

even if it's just not having the confidence to learn about the process and actually get to build your mobile site.

Not having the confidence in one's own capabilities is one of the most common challenges faced when business owners want to create a mobile-friendly website.

This is an easy challenge that's easy to overcome, as are the other biggest obstacles that commonly stand in a business owner's way.

Here's a breakdown of the biggest challenges, and how you can overcome them if they're what's standing in your way of unrealized profits.

How to Overcome the Challenge of Knowledge

While these may seem like two of the biggest obstacles, they go hand in hand. A business owner doesn't know the first thing about creating a website, let alone one that can be viewed on smartphones and mobile devices. This lack of know-how leads to them thinking that they are incompetent and incapable of building their own site and so, they don't even bother.

As a result of this lack of confidence their business suffers, because more people are using mobile browsers more and more often.

Solution: It's easy to say that the obvious solution is to have faith in yourself!

Yes, You Can!

Yes, of course that's a great answer, and a philosophy you should always carry it as a business owner. And, if it's simply a basic mobile website that you're looking for, it's also one that you should take with you when embarking on mobile website creation.

But when it comes to creating a more complex mobile website, the simple truth is that sometimes, a business owner simply can't do it. They don't have the time to create the site, they don't have the time to research how to do it, and they don't have the time to maintain it.

Even this should not shatter one's confidence, as there are many marketing consultants that do this every day, and have built a business around helping business owners create websites – mobile and otherwise.

When it comes to building a hugely complex e-commerce site with lots of content and lots of specialty plugins, coding and design options, all you as the business owner need to worry about is hiring the right one.

And surely you have the confidence in yourself to do that!

Challenge: I Don't Know What a Mobile Website Is

While just about every business owner today knows just how important it is to have a website for their customers to visit, many still aren't aware of the unrealized potential they are missing out on by not having a mobile website.

Many business owners don't even know what a mobile website is.

This is a huge problem, and one of the biggest when it comes to this type of business practice. When you don't know of the practice, you can't put it into place.

Solution: You're Already Solving the Problem!

By simply doing your research in reading this guide to building your mobile website, you're already learning how important it is to have one. Consider some of these stats and it will only reinforce why your business so badly needs a mobile website:

- "In the last few years, mobile search increased by 400%." – Google

- "9 out of 10 mobile searchers have taken action as a result of a smartphone search." – Google

- "Email activity on mobile devices accounts for 42% of US mobile Internet time." – The Nielsen Company

Now you know how important it is to have a mobile website for your business; and after reading this guide you'll also have the confidence and the know-how to do it.

First, let's look at the different types of mobile websites that you can have. From there, you'll be able to determine what tools you need to get started. Those resources could be anything as simple as a template, or as expansive as a marketing consultant, or team of them!

ABOUT THE AUTHOR

Jeff Collins has been an occasional ghost writer. He has written books on several subjects, ranging from self-help to economics.

Jeff is a graduate of journalism but he recently took on a Master's degree in Business Administration. The decision to study again came after the success of his affiliate marketing business. From there, he decided to branch off and find his own niche.

Today, Jeff works from the comforts of his home and frequently travels the world.